What Lovemaking
Means to
a Man

What Lovemaking Means to a Man

*Practical Advice
to Married Men
About Sex*

Tim and Beverly LaHaye

Zondervan Publishing House
Grand Rapids, Michigan

WHAT LOVEMAKING MEANS TO A MAN
Copyright © 1984 by The Zondervan Corporation

Zondervan Publishing House, 1415 Lake Drive, S.E.,
Grand Rapids, Michigan 49506

This book consists of two chapters taken from the larger book, *The Act
of Marriage*, copyright © 1976 by Tim and Beverly La Haye.

Library of Congress Cataloging in Publication Data

LaHaye, Tim F.
    What lovemaking means to a man.

    Bibliography: p.
    1. Sex instruction for men.   2. Men—Sexual behavior.
3. Sex in marriage.   4. Sex—Religious aspects—
Christanity.   I. LaHaye, Beverly.   II. Title.
HQ36.L26   1984   613.9'6   84-3546
ISBN 0-310-27102-9

Printed in the United States of America

84 85 86 87 88 89 90 / 10 9 8 7 6 5 4 3 2 1

*To all those who believe married love
can be beautiful, exciting, and fulfilling
and to those who wish
they could believe*

Contents

Introduction

"Self-preservation is the first law of life." With men, the sex drive is almost as powerful an instinct as self-preservation.

Sex is not evil. It is a gift of God our creator. Like everything else in life, there is a good use of sex as well as a misuse.

The Bible confines all expressions of sex to marriage. Anything outside of marriage is forbidden and condemned. But mutually satisfying love-making within marriage is the fulfillment of God's purpose in making us male and female.

Men and women are different, however, and the failure to understand this difference has caused great heartache and frustration to millions of men and women. They are not only different sexually and physically, but emotionally and mentally. This is important to realize, because satisfying sex in marriage involves every area of a person's life.

Sexual intercourse is the ultimate means of communication. Without words, it communicates an intimacy, identification, and companionship unshared on any other level. Next to one's spiritual communication with God, there is no more unifying means of communication between husband and wife than lovemaking. And the more each partner knows about what it means to his partner, the more effectively each may bring pleasure and satisfaction to the loved one.

This booklet contains three important chapters from my book *The Act of Marriage*, which will help men understand themselves and help wives understand their husbands. Most women rarely learn from a man's perspective what sex means from his point of view. This book will help women understand that complex sexual male with whom they will spend the rest of their life.

I hope you will take the time to read it carefully.

Author's note to men: If for some reason you find yourself becoming impotent on occasion or you have difficulty maintaining an erection, I have a special chapter for you in my book, *The Act of Marriage*, chapter 10, "The Impotent Man."

1

The Art of Lovemaking

Every significant physical activity in life is learned by practice; why should lovemaking be different? Adult human beings possess the desire and necessary equipment to make love, but the art of lovemaking is learned — it is not innate.

Dr. Ed Wheat of Springdale, Arkansas, told a group of men in a seminar, "If you do what comes naturally in lovemaking, almost every time you will be wrong." In reality he was cautioning his male audience that each "natural" or self-satisfying step in gaining sexual gratification for a man would probably be incompatible with his wife's needs. For that reason, a couple must seriously study this subject just prior to marriage, and then after their marriage they can begin their practice to learn satisfying techniques.

It is unrealistic to expect two virgins to reach simultaneous climaxes on the first night of their honeymoon. Research indicates that nine out of ten brides do not experience orgasm in intercourse on the first attempt. Obviously it would be ridiculous for a couple to feel they had failed each other because they happened to be in the ninety percentile. It is much more realistic for a couple to recognize that they must "learn by doing." Isn't that the primary purpose of a honeymoon — for two lovebirds to get away to a romantic spot and learn about each other and their sexual natures?

When intercourse is an expression of love, it can be enjoyable even when one or both partners do not experience an orgasm. The tenderness and intimate relationship may prove to give sufficient satisfaction in themselves. Naturally one must expect intense stimulation ultimately to culminate in orgasm for both, but that goal is not usually achieved immediately. Such a rewarding skill is learned after study, experimentation, and open communication between husband and wife.

The art of love that exists well within the capabilities of every couple reading this book will be presented in this chapter for honeymooners, even though it will probably be read by more married veterans than newlyweds. After all, the difference in lovemaking between virgins and experienced married partners is minor. One marriage counselor has advised, "If couples would treat each other all through marriage as they do on their honeymoon, they would have very few sex problems. But most experienced couples try to take short cuts, and that is what spoils their potential satisfaction."

THE ULTIMATE GOAL

Many pleasurable side effects arise from lovemaking, but we should not lose sight of the fact that the ultimate objective is orgasm for both the husband and wife. For the man this is usually quite simple and easily detected. When sufficient stimulation is applied to the nerve endings in the glans penis, a chain reaction is begun by creating muscular contractions in the prostrate gland, forcing the milky seminal fluid and sperm cells through the urethra with a force strong enough to ejaculate as far as twenty-four inches. Only then does the man realize that almost every organ and gland in his body has been brought into action, for after orgasm they all start to relax, and he becomes overwhelmed with a feeling of contentment.

The woman's orgasm is much more complex, and since she seems to be capable of several levels of climax, it is less obvious. For that reason, many young wives aren't sure whether they have reached an orgasm or not. Just as the gentle art of love has to be learned, so must she discern by personal experience what to expect of an orgasm. Once she has achieved a high-level orgasm, no longer does she doubt what it is or when it occurs.

With the goal of mutual orgasm before them, a couple is advised to take whatever time and steps are necessary to achieve that objective. Love, patience, unselfishness, concentration, and persistence place that goal well within the capability of every married couple!

PREPARATION FOR LOVE

One young bride-to-be interrupted me during my usual talk on intimate relationships before marrying a couple. "Pastor LaHaye, do we have to talk about this? It embarrasses me. It will work out by itself." No wonder that naive young lady became pregnant during the first month of marriage, and I would be surprised if she has yet learned sexual satisfaction.

Fortunately most brides expect to enjoy lovemaking and realistically face the fact that some preparation is necessary before they begin the actual experience. All such young people would be advised to consider the following minimal steps in that preparation:

1. Learn as much as you can before the wedding night. The previous chapter on sex education should be read several times to make sure both the bride and groom understand the functions of the male and female reproductive systems. We feel that the reading of this book and others listed at the close of the chapter should not be reviewed together until after the wedding. But both bride

and groom should read the basic material separately beforehand and then study it together on their honeymoon. This book is intended to be a help to such a couple on their wedding trip.

2. All prospective brides should visit their doctor several weeks before the wedding, discussing with him the advisability of breaking the hymen in the privacy of his office. If the doctor's examination shows that the hymen is thick and may obstruct sexual intercourse, she should consider letting him stretch it or cut it to avoid unnecessary pain and bleeding during intercourse. However, if the doctor feels she will have no serious difficulty and if the bride chooses, she may wish to leave it intact for her wedding night. In this enlightened age a bridegroom would rather have the hymen surgically removed in advance to reduce the possibility of causing pain to his virtuous young bride. Another alternative is digital stretching, which the husband can do on their wedding night, but this will require instructions from their doctor. In today's active world many virgins have broken the hymen in accidents while bicycling or horseback riding, or doctors may have had to dilate it because of menstrual difficulties.

The bride should discuss the matter of contraceptives with her doctor. We consider this in greater detail in chapter 11, but it is important for the bride and groom to realize that the fear of pregnancy can seriously detract from the joy of a honeymoon. The young couple should know each other's feelings and decide whether they are prepared to start a family right after marriage or not. If they plan on a short delay, the doctor can advise them on a good, safe contraceptive.

3. It is a rare bride who will be able to provide sufficient natural vaginal lubricant on her honeymoon to avoid painful sensations during the act of love. This possibility can be eliminated by securing a tube of surgical jelly from the druggist, or she may wish to discuss this with her doctor, who can prescribe an adequate preparation for

her. She would be advised to have it handy for her husband to use at the proper time.

4. The vaginal exercise program designed by Dr. Arnold Kegel is described in chapter 9. All brides-to-be should become aware of the muscles used and should practice Dr. Kegel's exercises several weeks before the wedding. The program will acquaint her with muscle control, about which most women know nothing, and in addition will magnify her potential sexual feeling during lovemaking. It will also provide her with a means of exciting her husband beyond his fondest dreams. Learning these exercises will further assist them in learning to reach simultaneous orgasms. The bride should carefully study chapter 9 on feminine response.

PRELIMINARY CONSIDERATIONS

We have noted that most women are more romantic than men. "Women are incurably romantic" came the comment from one analyst. Instead of fighting against that fact, the wise husband will cooperate with this need in his wife's heart. Because the honeymoon is the culmination of a girl's lifetime dreams, a loving husband will make every effort to fulfill them.

When I look back on our honeymoon, I have to admit that I planned everything wrong. Bev and I were married on a Saturday night in her home church. An old friend and his wife who came to the wedding decided to join us at our apartment while he gave me a one-hour lecture on the "facts of life." This took place after the reception, pictures, and packing of our car. We went to bed at 1:45 A.M.! Our first married day was spent driving for twelve hours, then stopping about 8 P.M. in a motel room somewhere in the mountains of Kentucky. The next day we arrived in Greenville, South Carolina, where another ministerial student and I were building a trailer court for married students. I promptly went back to work. About the only clear lesson Bev learned from that hectic trip was to begin adjusting immediately to the insane pace to which I have subjected her for twenty-eight exciting years.

If I had known then what I know now, I would have planned those few days after the wedding differently. First, we would have been married in the afternoon. Then we would have slipped away from our friends to be alone, planning at least a week to get acquainted before my bride was confronted with her new life style as a wife.

One of the chief advantages of an afternoon wedding is having an entire first night without the fomenting turmoil that inevitably awaits a young couple after the reception. They need to get away to a hotel room to retire, unpack, freshen up, and leisurely enjoy a snack or dinner together. Most young people eat and sleep erratically before their wedding and, due to the frenzy of preparations, leave the ceremony totally exhausted. They need to sit down quietly, relax from all the excitement, and eat enough to lift their blood sugar level for added energy.

Upon returning to the room, the bridegroom may wish to carry his bride over the threshold in the traditional manner. From this point on, the two of them will be alone and should feel free to become as intimately acquainted as possible. The husband should proceed slowly and very gently with tender caresses and verbal expressions of love. There is a thin line at this stage between a husband's love and a man's passion. The husband who hurries this first encounter may unconsciously convey the thought to his new wife that he is being driven by passion more than love and concern for her. A slow, gentle approach will reveal his love for her through self-control.

It is important to add here that all lovemaking should proceed in circumstances where the couple can be guaranteed absolute privacy. Men are so single-minded that this is not so important to them as to their wives, but modest women need the assurance that no one will accidentally interrupt them. In a motel room it is easy to fasten the night lock. In their bedroom at home, they should install a lock on the door. Such a precaution is a necessary investment for successful lovemaking.

The romantic-minded husband will see to it that lights are turned low, thus ensuring visibility without excessive brightness, and if possible provide soft music.

THE GREAT UNVEILING

At this point the husband must be very sensitive to the romantic fantasies of his wife. Some brides will succumb to the lingerie industry's commercials and wear a sexy nightie bought especially for the honeymoon. If so, she may want to slip into the bathroom to make the change. However, the couple may wish to stir sexual excitement for love by undressing one another. The lover finds it terribly exciting and stimulating to be gently undressed by his loved one. Although one may experience some embarrassment at being fully unclothed before his partner the first time, such a feeling will be minimal and will soon dissolve if the undressing proceeds slowly, even in stages, with tender, compassionate expressions of love. When the husband assures his modest bride that she is truly the most beautiful creature he has ever seen, she will most likely respond with a warm embrace.

FOREPLAY

Almost every sex manual emphasizes the need for an adequate period of foreplay, or loveplay. This is true not only on the first night, but all through marriage. Most men have learned that foreplay is essential to their wives' enjoyment of lovemaking, but they generally minimize their own need because they are fully aroused for lovemaking at the sight of their beloved's nude body. Yet current research has revealed that it is easier for a man to retard his ejaculation after a long period of foreplay than after sudden arousal. Besides, as he learns how affectionately to arouse his wife, he will attain in her response intense excitement himself, and it will enrich his own climax.

How long the couple should spend in foreplay may vary with each couple's need, depending somewhat upon their temperaments and cultural background. But it is never wise to be in a hurry. A modest, inexperienced bride may require thirty or more minutes in preparation for lovemaking. After she becomes more experienced, the preparatory time may be reduced to ten or fifteen minutes; occasional exceptions during her emotional cycle when she is particularly amorous may reduce the time even further.

There is no universal pattern for arousing a woman to lovemaking. Some women are stimulated by having their breasts caressed, others are not. Furthermore, a woman's emotional cycle may make it enjoyable for her on some occasions, but not on others. For this reason, a wife should freely instruct her husband through verbal responses and by placing his hands where she wants him to caress her tenderly. Generally a thoughtful husband may gently massage his wife's neck, shoulders, and breasts to arouse her until blood rushes to the nipples and they become firm and erect, though care should be taken not to irritate the nipples by too vigorous action. Any tender fondling and kissing on the upper body will help to arouse her. Gradually the husband should move his hands gently down his wife's body until he contacts the vulva region, mindful to keep his fingernails smoothly filed to avoid producing any discomfort (which could cause her heating emotions to become suddenly chilled).

As the husband is tenderly caressing the clitoris or vaginal area with his hand, the couple will probably be lying on the bed with the wife on her back. If she will spread her legs, keeping her feet flat on the bed, and pull them up toward her body, it will be helpful for them both. The husband finds this voluntary act of cooperation very exciting, and it makes her most sensitive areas accessible to his caressing fingers. It is best for the husband to fondle the area around the clitoris, but he should not start foreplay there at first because of potential irritation. As the area starts to engorge with blood, it becomes the primary source of excitement to the wife and is then ready for direct stimulation.

On first arousal the husband will be able to feel the clitoris with his fingers, but his wife will go through several physiological changes as her excitement mounts. Her heart will palpitate, her skin become warm, and almost every part of her body become sensitive to the touch. Her breathing will be more rapid, her face may grimace as if in pain, and she may groan audibly — and her husband finds this all very exhilarating. The most noticeable change will take place in the vaginal area, where she becomes very moist and the inner lips (labia minora) begin to swell several times their normal size until they form a hood over the clitoris, which may no longer be felt by his fingers. At this point it usually becomes unnecessary to maintain direct contact with the clitoris, for any motion in the vaginal region will vibrate against the thick layers of the swollen hood and transmit the movements to the clitoris indirectly. This will further amplify passion in the wife.

The vigor with which the husband massages this vital area should be determined by the wife. Some prefer it slow and easy, while others enjoy vigorous motion. Some wives like to vary the motion within one lovemaking experience; others may choose to modify it according to their mood. Most important, the husband should be extremely gentle and sensitive to his wife's needs at this point.

The mounting passions and tensions in a wife at this stage can be likened to pushing a cart uphill. As one gradually approaches the top, the peak seems to become steeper; then with a final thrust, the cart can be pushed over the top. Just as one would never stop the cart on the uphill side, so a thoughtful husband will not suspend his motion in the midst of their loveplay. If he does, her emotional cart will *immediately* descend and he will have to regain the emotional loss. This explains why many women cool somewhat during the time it takes a husband to remove his fingers from her vaginal area and place his penis inside, particularly if he has any clothing to remove. With practice he can learn to continue the massaging loveplay while putting the penis into place. This will help his wife continue her climb toward a high emotional peak. After the husband learns more self-control, he may stimulate his wife's clitoris with a lubricated penis. Some wives may prefer this to the husband's fingers. Then it is easily slipped into the vagina when she is ready.

THE CULMINATION

Many an inexperienced husband misunderstands a very important signal from his wife. When his fingers are caressing the vaginal area and he finds it well lubricated, he may consider that to be the signal that she is ready for coitus. This is not true!! Until her labia minora are heavily swollen by the influx of an ample supply of blood, the sensitive areas of her vagina will not even be included in their lovemaking. If he proceeds before that, he will probably reach orgasm just as this swelling takes place, and she will be left unfulfilled. His relaxing penis will then be unable to continue the motion on the sides of the vagina and the clitoris necessary to bring her to climax. This common misunderstanding probably has kept more loving partners from learning to reach simultaneous orgasms than anything else.

The husband must also remember when massaging the area of the vagina and clitoris that at first touch with dry fingers his wife might experience some discomfort. If he moistens his finger with vaginal lubrication, she will find clitoral stimulation much more enjoyable. Free and honest communication is essential in this phase of loveplay to maximize the enjoyment of this necessary preparation for the act of marriage.

Several writers in this field, both Christian and secular, suggest that a couple gently massage each other to orgasm on their wedding night for two reasons: (1) it increases the possibility for both to experience an orgasm the first night, and (2) it helps to acquaint them with their partner's bodily functions. We believe this might be a little too much to expect from two inhibited virgins their first night together. We suggest, however, that they arouse each other as outlined above, and when the wife thinks she is ready for entrance, she should take the groom's penis in her hand and place it in her vagina. Upon his wife's signal and while continuing to massage her clitoral area, the husband should use his free hand to take a lubricating jelly (which should be placed on the night-stand in advance) and lubricate the head and shaft of his penis before entrance. He should be careful to support the weight of his body with his elbows and slowly push his penis into her vagina.

Once inside, the husband should try to remain motionless or he may ejaculate in a matter of seconds, abruptly terminating their lovemaking. Even though all his instincts cry out within him to begin his thrusting motion, he must gain self-control for at least one or two minutes. To avoid the loss of his wife's mounting tension, he should continue to massage her clitoral area or the swollen lips of the vulva. The wife can help to increase her passion by slightly rotating her hips as she lies beneath her husband. This helps to maintain motion and friction on her clitoris and bring her vagina into contact with the shaft of his penis without overstimulating him. When she feels her passions mounting beyond control, she should put her legs around her husband's hips and begin her own thrusting movements back and forth on the penis. If she has practiced contracting the vaginal (P.C.) muscle several weeks before marriage as described in chapter 9, she will find more pleasure in the experience and can help her husband by squeezing his penis with the muscle each time he retracts. A squeezing action upon first entry is also helpful to both husband and wife — while the husband is waiting one to two minutes for ejaculatory control, his wife's squeezing can maintain her excitement. Once the husband begins his thrusting motion, the wife should concentrate on the sensations she is experiencing in her clitoris and vaginal area, continuing as much motion as possible that contributes to that feeling.

The husband, no matter how inexperienced, will intuitively recognize his wife's accelerated motion as the signal for him to begin his thrusting motion, and he will likely expel his mixture of seminal fluid and sperm cells into her vagina within just a few thrusts. He should continue thrusting after his ejaculation as long as he can in case his wife's orgasm is all but seconds behind his.

Shortly after ejaculation, his penis will lose its rigidity and will no longer maintain sufficient friction on the vagina walls and labia minora to increase his wife's excitement. If she has not reached an orgasm during their first coitus, the young lovers should not feel discouraged. The husband can immediately begin manual stimulation of his wife's clitoris and vulva area, as he did in foreplay, to help bring her to orgasm. Although it is possible for a bride to experience orgasm during the couple's first encounter, it is unusual, especially for a virgin.

THE AFTERGLOW

Most brides find their initial lovemaking, when preceded by sufficient loveplay, a delightfully exciting experience even without orgasm. The free experimentation with their beloved's nude body is stimulating, unsurpassed by any previous experience. Even such pain as she may have felt in the breaking of her hymen or the possible stretching of the vagina will usually be eclipsed by the stimulation of areas she has never used before. Many wives have indicated that the blast of their lover's warm seminal fluid inside the vagina is also thrilling. Coupled with the intimate closeness of their entwined bodies, this makes it a most enjoyable expression of love. If her orgasm was not achieved, her emotional tension will gradu-

22

ally subside and her reproductive organs, like those of her husband, will slowly return to normal.

There is no need for lovers to withdraw immediately after completion of intercourse. We advise that they remain in each other's embrace for several minutes and continue to exchange caresses. Many couples fall asleep in this position or learn to roll onto their sides, the limp penis gradually sliding out of the vagina. Their physical and emotional exhaustion generally produces a deep, satisfying slumber.

It usually takes the husband forty-five minutes to an hour or more before he can be ready for lovemaking again. This is not true of the wife. Research by Masters and Johnson indicates that a woman can experience several orgasms, one right after another.[1] For that reason, whenever a wife is brought to orgasm by her husband's hand during foreplay, he should continue to massage her vaginal and clitoral area, for she will soon regain the feeling of mounting excitement and can repeat the orgasmic experience. It may be difficult for a man to understand how his wife can immediately be ready for more when he is powerless to regain his sex drive without a period of rest, but she is suprisingly capable of continuing orgasms. In fact, some women have reported that their most powerful climaxes are sometimes their fourth or fifth in a lovemaking session. However, if the husband stops his stimulation of the clitoris and vaginal area immediately after the first orgasm, she will gradually lose her mounting passion and retreat to a state of emotional and physical exhaustion similar to that of her husband.

HONEYMOON EXPERIMENTATION

Honeymoons exist not only to provide a special time for companionship, but to promote sexual learning and experimentation. For that reason, couples should try various methods of stimulation, positions (see pages 82-84), times of day, and whatever they both find enjoyable. We recommend that sometime during their honeymoon, in order to understand fully their partner's physiological function during lovemaking, they bring each other to orgasm by hand. This experiment should be carried out in a lighted room where they may be free from any interruptions. Unclothed, they should maintain the same romantic atmosphere and unhurried preparation as for any other period of lovemaking.

It is advisable that the husband try to bring his wife to orgasm first, because after his climax it is usually difficult for him to be vitally interested in lovemaking for some time. Proceeding in the manner outlined above, he should lie on his side next to and slightly above his wife while he tenderly caresses the clitoris and the vaginal area with his hand. When the labia minora are sufficiently swollen, indicating that she is responding properly and her vagina is well lubricated, he will feel that the protective hood has covered the clitoris area, and he can create friction in both places at once. She may want him to insert one finger very gently into the vagina, making slow rhythmic movements inside while his other fingers continue contact with the outer vulval area. This will usually give her a delightful sensation and help to increase her excitement. She should feel free to use her hand to guide her husband's to the most responsive areas and create the most stimulating motions. Then she should concentrate with abandon on those vital areas of friction and let herself go completely, so that if she wishes to groan, cry, wiggle, rotate, or thrust, she may do so.

To realize fully her capability after her first orgasm, the wife should encourage her husband to slacken his motions, but not discontinue them. As her excitement begins to mount again, she can signal him to speed up his motion and increase its vigor to her satisfaction until she reaches another orgasm. Twice will probably be sufficient at this state of their marriage.

After her climax, the wife should turn on her side while the husband lies on his back. Gently massaging the genital region, she should run her fingers over his penis, pubic hair, scrotum, and inner thighs. She should be very careful not to put pressure on his testicles located inside his scrotal sac, as this can be quite uncomfortable. With her hand around the shaft of the penis, she should begin massaging up and down. As her motion becomes more rapid, her husband's body will grow more rigid, and she will be able to verify his response to her touch. This motion should be continued until he ejaculates. Before beginning this exercise, the wife should have several tissues on hand to absorb the discharge. Afterward she can observe how rapidly her husband's penis returns to normal.

Dr. Herbert J. Miles, in his excellent book *Sexual Happiness in Marriage*, tells the following story:

> One couple in the research sample had this experience. They attempted intercourse on their wedding night and the wife did not have an orgasm, but the husband did. After intercourse, they attempted to bring her to an orgasm by direct stimulation. In the process she gradually became tense, nervous, and just could not continue the arousal effort, although she tried and wanted to do so. She had to ask her husband to stop the stimulation. They lay there, relaxed, and talked for over three hours, on into the night. Finally, long after midnight she said, "I want us to try that again." They repeated the process of direct stimulation and after about seventeen minutes she reached her first orgasm. What actually happened, in her case, was that she learned much in her first effort and after becoming relaxed and more confident, she was able to give herself fully to sexual arousal and thus succeeded.[2]

Some Christians might object to this form of experimentation. We recommend it for newlyweds, because they are building a lifetime relationship together in which lovemaking will play a permanent role for up to sixty years. The more they know about each other by personal experience, the more they will enjoy each other and more likely experience what we consider the ultimate in lovemaking: simultaneous orgasms most of the time. This form of "learning by doing" will increase the likelihood that they will learn the art early in marriage and go on to enjoy it for many years. Part of the therapy recommended by Masters and Johnson for sexual dysfunction is this same experimentation. Couples married for years have been helped to a better understanding of each other and a better sexual relationship through this kind of learning process.

Dr. Miles suggests, "There are three steps in sexual adjustment that couples need to learn. They are as follows: first step — orgasms, second step — orgasms in intercourse, third step — orgasms together or close together in intercourse."[3]

A couple should not be discouraged if they do not achieve the second or third step right away. It may take several weeks or longer before they can experience simultaneous orgasms on a regular basis. However, it should be a goal for which every couple strives.

Another area in which a couple will want to experiment is positions for most effective sexual arousal. One of the most convenient has the wife lying on her back with knees bent and feet pulled up to her hips and her husband lying on her right side. Dr. Miles explains what the Bible says about a married couple's position for lovemaking.

This position of sexual arousal is described in the Bible in the Song of Solomon 2:6 and 8:3. These two verses are identical. They read as follows: "Let his left hand be under my head and his right hand embrace me." The word "embrace" could be translated "fondle" or "stimulate." Here in the Bible, in a book dealing with pure married love, a married woman expresses herself with longing that her husband put his left arm under her head and that he uses his right hand to stimulate her clitoris.

This position of sexual arousal seems to have been the position used by many people back through the centuries. We do not hesitate to say that the general arousal procedure described here is a part of the plan of God as

He created man and woman. Therefore, mankind has used this procedure because it is the plan of God and because it is efficient.[4]

Dr. Miles further gives some sound advice regarding the extent of intimacy between the husband and wife.

> In interpersonal relationships in the community and society, modesty is a queen among virtues, but in the privacy of the marriage bedroom, behind locked doors, and in the presence of pure married love, there is no such thing as modesty. A couple should feel free to do whatever they both enjoy which moves them into a full expression of their mutual love and in a sexual experience.
>
> At this point it is well to give a word of caution. *All sex experiences should be those which both husband and wife want.* Neither, at any time, should force the other to do anything that he does not want to do. Love does not force.[5]

One characteristic of the Holy Spirit is love, and a dominant trait of love is kindness. The intimacy of lovemaking should always be performed with kindness. At times vigorous activity is required, but it will always be expressed in kindness to the other person — a vital evidence that the act of marriage is in reality an act of love.

CLITORAL STIMULATION

The reluctance of many loving partners to incorporate clitoral stimulation as a necessary and meaningful part of their foreplay has probably cheated more women out of the exciting experience of orgasmic fulfillment than any other one thing. Because it has often been associated with self-stimulation, even some husbands are unaware of how essential a part of the lovemaking process it is.

To highlight the significance of the clitoris to the woman's sexual enjoyment, many researchers have compared it with the penis. It has been called the "most keenly sexual part of a woman's body" and is still regarded by many "as the seat of all sexual satisfaction."[6]

R.M. Deutsch has stated that "stimulation of the clitoris alone will produce an orgasm in nearly all women . . . . direct clitoral stimulation alone [will] produce the climax."[7] He further indicates that "most researchers agree that the clitoris, unlike any male organ, has only one purpose — sexual stimulation."[8]

Another researcher indicates that the clitoris has the same number of nerve endings as does the penis, but is only one-tenth the size. Therefore it is the culmination in feminine sexual capability. To disregard it is to guarantee feminine orgasmic malfunction or incapability.

From a practical standpoint it has no bearing on reproduction and is unnecessary for any other female function. Thus it is safe to conclude that God designed it to be used in lovemaking. It could well be that the thrilling response of the wife referred to in the Song of Solomon 5:4 may allude to the husband's use of clitoral manipulation. Such foreplay is not only acceptable behavior by married partners, but also was designed by God as one of the most delightful aspects of the act of marriage.

THE FOUR PHASES OF SEXUAL AROUSAL

Modern research, particularly that of Masters and Johnson, acquaints us with four distinct phases of sexual arousal for both male and female: (1) the excitement phase, (2) the plateau phase, (3)the orgasmic phase, and (4) the resolution phase. Admittedly, reducing all human responses to a single chart does not allow for individual variation, and from that standpoint it oversimplifies the matter, but it does provide a basic pattern upon which to establish a norm. As noted in the following diagrams, only one characteristic response of men is indicated, whereas three are listed for women. The male response is more prone to be basic, whereas women tend to reflect more individual variation. In addition, because of the greater complexity of a woman's orgasmic function, she may experience each of these responses throughout

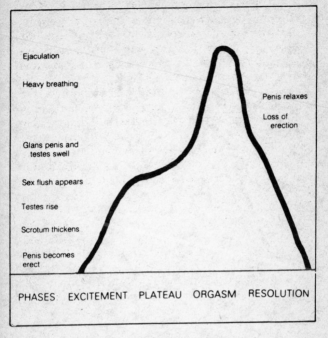

Fig. 3. Sexual response of the husband

her married life as she is learning the art of love expression.

On the wife's chart we have distinguished the three responses as (A) the multiple orgasm, the ideal she would like to achieve; (B) the orgasmic failure, the sexual response that far too many settle for (a failure that often can be changed by a little more understanding, added foreplay, and increased tenderness on the part of her companion; and (C) the single orgasm, probably the most frequent expression of the well-adjusted married woman who may reserve the multiple experience for special occasions when her mood, time allotted for lovemaking, and other factors fall into place.

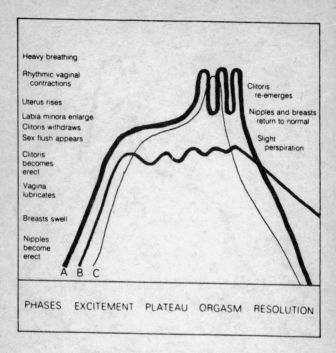

Heavy breathing

Rhythmic vaginal
  contractions

Uterus rises

Labia minora enlarge

Clitoris withdraws

Sex flush appears

Clitoris
becomes
erect

Vagina
lubricates

Breasts swell

Nipples
become
erect

Clitoris
re-emerges

Nipples and breasts
return to normal

Slight
perspiration

A   B   C

PHASES   EXCITEMENT   PLATEAU   ORGASM   RESOLUTION

Fig. 4 Sexual response of the wife

As the chart indicates a certain physiological changes take place in each stage. These should be studied and lovers should experiment to the point of learning what to expect in each of these phases.

VARIOUS POSITIONS

Since the earliest days of writing various lovemaking positions have been recorded. One author claims there are ninety-nine different positions. The trouble with about ninety-five of them is that only a gymnast could enjoy them. Actually there are only four positions used frequently enough to consider here. Dr. Miles shares his research findings on the first three.

1. The husband above

Our research indicates that 91 percent of couples use the man above position all of the time or most all of the time. Fifty-four percent of couples experiment frequently with other positions, but usually finish with the man above position. Only 4 percent use some position other than the man above position more than half of the time, and only 5 percent use some other position all of the time.

It is important to the husband to have his feet firmly against the foot of the bed or some solid object to aid him in giving full expression to his sexual orgasm. In case of a bed that has no foot-board, the couple may reverse their position, placing his feet against the head-board.

2. The wife above

The wife above position allows the husband to relax and control himself, and permits the wife to initiate the movement necessary to give her the most stimulation by forcing the clitoris to move over the penis. The disadvantages are that this position is often not comfortable for the wife, the husband may have difficulty in controlling his arousal, and neither are in proper position to give fullest expression during orgasms. For some couples the advantages outweigh the disadvantages. This position is often advantageous for a large husband and a small wife.

3. Both on their sides

Another useful position is for both husband and wife to lie on their sides facing the same direction with the husband back of the wife. The penis is moved into the vaginal passage from the rear. The disadvantages are that the penis cannot contact the clitoris and the couple cannot kiss during the experience. The advantages are that the position is very comfortable, the husband can easily use his fingers to stimulate his wife's clitoris, and he can control his own arousal. There are other slight variations of this approach. Many couples use this position for the arousal period and shift quickly to the man above position for orgasms.[9]

4. Husband seated.

Depending on their comparative heights, a couple may sometimes enjoy the position of the husband seated on a low couch or backless chair. The wife can lower herself onto his penis at her discretion. This position is good for those wives who find that the entrance of the male organ is painful. By controlling the entrance, a wife can minimize the pain. Such sensations will be short-lived, and couples should not give up or use pain as an excuse to avoid lovemaking permanently. If pain is not eliminated by application of generous amounts of lubricant, see your physician.

Most couples experiment with these and other positions, but most return to the man above. It seems to be the most satisfying to the largest number of lovers.

SUMMARY

The art of mutually enjoyable lovemaking is not difficult to learn, but neither is it automatic. No one is a good lover by nature, and thus the more selfish the individual, the more difficulty he will have learning this art. If two people love each other with an unselfish love and are willing to control themselves while seeking to learn how to render emotional and physical satisfaction to their partner, they will learn. It does, however, demand time and practice. Any individual taking time to read this book has indicated he is concerned enough to try. Dr. Ed Wheat has sagely said, "Every physical union should be a contest to see which partner can outplease the other."

With this concept in mind, I told a story in the chapter on "Physical Adjustment" in my book *How to Be Happy Though Married.* It was given to me by a minister friend who had counseled a frustrated couple in the art of clitoral stimulation so that in a very brief period of time they resolved their problem.

Four months after that book was published, I was speaking at a banquet in a very small city in northern California. A dentist shared with me privately that he had read the book and had been reminded of his own case. When he related his story, I found it an exciting corollary to the earlier tale.

The young dentist and his wife of three years were deeply in love, but his wife had never reached orgasm during their marriage. He found this almost as frustrating as she did. As a dentist, he had studied anatomy and felt that he knew more than the average person about the functions of the human body. This knowledge, however, did not seem to resolve their difficulty, and their sexual frustration soon produced marital conflict. Since they were not Christians at the time, they decided to start going to church as a last resort to save their marriage. They fortunately selected a gospel-preaching church, and in about three months they both had accepted Christ as their personal Lord and Savior. But this still did not resolve their problem of orgasmic malfunction.

One Sunday morning their pastor was preaching on the text, "In all thy ways acknowledge Him, and He shall direct thy paths." They heard him say, "You do not have a problem in your life that you cannot take to the Lord in prayer." The dentist looked at his wife and realized that they had not prayed about it. Afterward they discussed it and decided to do so.

On Friday of that week they were invited to a social gathering. Being the first to arrive, they were ushered into the family room to await the arrival of the other guests. It was a large room with a couple of conversation areas, so they chose a couch on the far side of the room. They were no sooner seated than another couple came in and sat on the first couch behind them, a large floral arrangement preventing them from being seen by the new arrivals. Thinking they were alone, this sanguine husband put his arm around his wife and exclaimed, "Hasn't our relationship been beautiful since we discovered clitoral stimulation?" The dentist silently glanced at his wife and thought, "We have never tried that." That night they did, and it was the beginning of a new experience for them both.

With obvious emotion the dentist told me, "That simple technique was like a key that opened the door to a beautiful relationship which we have enjoyed for the past three years."

This story shows evidence of God's abundant grace. In a small town without counselors, and under the ministry of a young, single seminary student, this young couple told their heavenly Father of their need and sought His help. He guided them to the right place at the right time to hear the information He wanted them to know.

No one has a problem that cannot be taken to his heavenly Father. No one need settle for a lifetime of sexual frustration. When God's children pray for His guidance and His will for their lives, He is always faithful in revealing it to them. This relationship with God will bless the lives and strengthen the faith of those who trust in Him for help.

Notes

[1] William H. Masters and Virginia E. Johnson, *Human Sexual Response* (Boston: Little, Brown and Co., 1966), p. 131.

[2] Herbert J. Miles, *Sexual Happiness in Marriage* (Grand Rapids: Zondervan Publishing House, 1967), p. 96.

[3] Ibid., p. 97.

[4] Ibid., p. 79.

[5] Ibid., p. 78.

[6] Ronald M. Deutsch, *The Key to Feminine Response in Marriage* (New York: Random House, 1968), p. 39.

2

What Lovemaking Means
to a Man

Viewing life through someone else's eyes is a key to communication on any level. The failure of many wives to understand what lovemaking really means to a man often leads to an erroneous conclusion that stifles her natural ability to respond to his advances.

Susie began our counseling interview by grumbling, "Our problem is — Bill is a beast! All he ever thinks of is sex, sex, sex! Ever since I met him it seems I've been fighting him off. Maybe he's oversexed!" What kind of man do you envision after hearing her description of Bill? Probably a copper-skinned giant with virility exuding from every pore of his body and elevator eyes that flirt with every pretty girl who comes along. Nothing could be further from the truth! Bill is a quiet, dependable, hard-working, affectionate family man in his late twenties who is still a little insecure. When I asked how often they made love, she replied, "Three or four times a week." (We have discovered that wives usually report more frequent lovemaking experiences than their husbands, and a dissatisfied husband usually underestimates the frequency of their experiences. By averaging their reports, we gain a more accurate figure). Actually Bill is not abnormal; in fact, our survey and others find him functioning well within the range of the average husband at his age.

Susie had three problems: she did not like sexual relations, she did not understand Bill's needs, and she was more interested in herself than her husband. When she confessed her sin of selfishness and learned what loving really meant to him, it changed their bedroom life. Today she enjoys lovemaking, and recently she dropped us a thank-you note for the time we had spent with her, concluding, "Would you believe the other night Bill said, 'Honey, what's come over you? For years I chased you around the bed, and now you're chasing me!'" Doubtless, she did not have to chase him very far.

The act of marriage is vitally significant to the husband for at least five different reasons:

1. *It satisfies his sex drive.* It is usually agreed that the male in all species of living creatures has the stronger sex drive, and Homo sapiens is no exception. That does not suggest that women lack a strong sex drive, but as we shall see in the next chapter, hers is sporadic whereas his is almost continual.

God designed man to be the aggressor, provider, and leader of his family. Somehow that is tied to his sex drive. The woman who resents her husband's sex drive while enjoying his aggressive leadership had better face the fact that she cannot have one without the other.

To illustrate the physical cause of the male sex drive, let us introduce the scientific evidence that "each drop of (seminal) fluid is said to contain as many as 300 million sperm."[1] Since it is possible for a man to have two to five ejaculations a day, depending upon his age, it is obvious that his reproductive system manufactures a supply of semen and many millions of tiny sperm daily. If unreleased through coitus, this can be very frustrating to his mental and physical well-being. One writer has said, "A normal and healthy man has a semen build-up every 42 to 78 hours that produces a pressure that needs to be released." A variety of conditions will determine the frequency of that pressure. For example, if psychological work or family problems weigh upon his mind, he will not be as vitally conscious of that pressure as when he is relaxed. Studies have indicated that men from rural areas consistently desire coitus more frequently than do men from urban areas in the same age brackets. Researchers explain that this occurs because urbanites tend to undergo more psychological pressures than their rural counterparts. One other possibility, however, is that rural men of all ages tend to work harder physically and thus are probably in better physical condition than their urban counterparts, who may enjoy a more sedentary life.

One of the most common misconceptions in the minds of young married women pertains to the sexual needs of their husbands. Due to their lack of experience, preconceived notions, and most of all their fear of pregnancy, many young wives do not share their husbands' enthusiasm for lovemaking. This trend seems to reverse itself later in the marriage, but in the earlier years the frequency of sex is often cause for conflict and disagreement. Young wives may equate their husbands' youthful passion with bestiality, not realizing that their husbands' drives are not unique, but characteristic of most normal men. These drives are the gift of God to produce the motivation for procreation which is still the primary social purpose of mankind. That gift not only influences his sexual behavior, but also his personality, work, motivation, and almost every other characteristic in his life. Without it he would not be the man with whom she fell in love. It is a wise woman who cooperates with that need rather than fights against it.

2. *It fulfills his manhood.* A man usually possesses a stronger ego than a woman. If he is not a man in his own eyes, he is nothing; and somehow his sex drive seems to be intricately linked to his ego. I have never met an impotent or sexually frustrated man who enjoyed a strong self-image. A sexually satisfied husband is a man who will rapidly develop self-confidence in other areas of his life.

Most men do not blame their insecurities on sexual frustration because they are either too proud or do not realize the connection; but I have observed it so often that whenever I find a fractured male ego, I look for sexual frustration. A man can endure academic, occupational, and social failure as long as he and his wife relate well together in the bedroom; but success in other fields becomes a hollow mockery if he strikes out in bed. To the man, being unsuccessful in his bedroom signals failure in life.

One loving wife asked what she could do for her husband whose business had just collapsed. He was more depressed than she had ever seen him before, and she felt incapable of reaching him. "I'm confident he will bounce back," she said. "He's too dynamic a man to let this one failure ruin his whole life." Since she had already prayed with him and committed their economic future to God, I suggested that she make aggressive love to him, that she dress provocatively and use her feminine charm to seduce him. She spontaneously asked, "Don't you think he'll get suspicious? He's always been the aggressor in that department." Her response gave me an opportunity to explain that his fractured ego needed the reassurance of her love during a time of defeat. Many husbands subconsciously fear that their wives endure lovemaking out of a sense of duty or some lesser motivation. What every man needs, especially during a period of defeat, is to be convinced that his wife loves him for himself, not for anything he does for her. I knew her dynamic, choleric husband well enough to perceive that he was not complicated enough to get suspicious; any surprise would give way to ecstasy. Later his wife reported that he not only lacked suspicion, but within five minutes after lovemaking began to share a new business idea with her. Although that idea never materialized, it started him upward. He soon found his niche and today is enjoying a successful career.

One instructive aspect of this case is the fact that her husband now credits his wife with helping him "bounce back." He never refers to their lovemaking experience, of course, but says such things as "My wife is quite a gal! When I was down and out, she still had faith in me. It was her confidence that sparked my own." Actually, before she ever came to me, she had verbalized her confidence in him many times by such expressions as "Don't let it get you down; you can start over again." But not until she made love to him did she communicate her confidence in terms that he could understand. Much later she offered a rather interesting comment to me: she could not remember her husband ever holding her so tightly during lovemaking. But that is not really difficult to understand. Men are just boys grown tall, and this man's failure had shaken his manhood and accentuated the boy that lurks in the heart of every man. But love once again succeeded when all else failed.

Some women will probably take exception to this use of lovemaking as another example of the "exploitation of sex." We prefer to think of it as the expression of unselfish love. Because of her love for her husband, this wife created an atmosphere on the basis of her husband's need, not his feelings — nor hers, for that matter. It is a beautiful fulfillment of the Bible's description of love: "Look not every man on his own things [needs], but every man also on the things [needs] of others" (Phil. 2:4).

One woman shared with us, "No matter what our love life consists of, there is one time each month when I always try to get my husband to make love to me — the night after he has paid the family bills. It seems to be the only thing that gets him back to normal." Her husband gets an *F* for failing to commit his problems to God and learning to rejoice by faith (1 Thess. 5:18), but she rates an *A* for being a wise and loving wife.

These stories appear in stark contrast to what usually goes on when hubby's ego is flattened by failure, debt, or problems. Most self-centered wives are so "shaken" by the sight of an insecure husband during a period of testing that they are ill-prepared to be a husband's "helpmeet" during the time of his distress. Do not be deceived by that thin coating of tough masculinity most men wear; underneath are many emotional needs that only a loving wife can supply.

The old Victorian nonsense that a "nice lady doesn't act as if she enjoys sex" conflicts with a good husband's need to know that his wife thoroughly enjoys his lovemaking. The Victorians did not seem to distinguish between their premarital and marital taboos. Naturally a good, wholesome Christian woman will not flaunt her enjoyment of sex; that is a personal matter. Far too many insecure women are tricked into thinking that they should look and act sexy in public. That is distorted sex appeal! A truly secure woman will convey her sex appeal and satisfaction only to her husband. It gives him great pleasure and, in fact, makes his own sexual pleasure much more satisfying when he is assured that it has been mutually enjoyed. A wise and considerate woman goes out of her way to let her man know that he is a good lover and that she enjoys their relations together. It is good for his ego and promotes honest communication between them. Only a false and insincere modesty would hide such vital knowledge from a partner. Genuine love flourishes in giving. That is why a devoted husband finds great delight in knowing his wife enjoys his lovemaking.

The benefits of such love not only intensify the solidarity of the lovers, but spill over and bless the children. A secure man becomes a better father, uses better judgment, and improves his capacity to love the entire family.

3. *It enhances his love for his wife.* We are familiar with the word *syndrome,* but we usually associate it with negative things like depression, anger, or fear. However, it is appropriately used in conjunction with love. A love syndrome never hurt anyone, and such a syndrome is created between married partners when their lovemaking is mutually satisfying.

Because a man has been endowed by God with an intense sex drive and a conscience, the satisfactory release of that drive without provoking his conscience will enhance his love for the person who makes that possible. But only one person on earth can do that — his wife.

Follow our reasoning. A man's sex drive can be relieved only by ejaculation. This can be achieved by (1) intercourse, (2) masturbation, (3) nocturnal emission, or (4) homosexuality. Intercourse is beyond comparison the most satisfying means of ejaculation, but this in turn can be accomplished by the act of marriage, by prostitution, òr by adultery. Only one of these, however, is accompanied by a clear conscience — married love. Our chapter of questions and answers (chapter 14) will deal with illegitimate sexual experiences, but here it must be pointed out that they all have one factor in common. Though they provide biological release, they do not guarantee lasting enjoyment, because the conscience God has given to every man "accuses" him when he violates divine standards of morality (read Rom. 1). When sex provides only gratification and is followed by guilt, it makes a mockery of what God intended to be a very satisfying experience. By contrast, the act of marriage when properly performed is followed by physical relaxation based on innocence. Because sex is such a necessary part of a man's life and married love preserves the innocence of his conscience, the woman who provides these for him will increasingly become the object of his love.

Bobbie was a typical southern belle who came for counseling because she felt Joe didn't love her any more. Although she couldn't prove it, she charged, "I'm sure he's seeing another woman." It seemed incredible that any man would look elsewhere when he had such a beautiful wife with so charming an accent. But under questioning, it turned out that she had been using sex as a reward, rationing it out only on Joe's good behavior. Like any normal man, Joe found that intolerable. We may never know whether he was actually unfaithful, for after some straightforward talk in the counseling room, Bobbie went home to love her husband unconditionally. At first he was stunned to find his wife sexually aggressive, but in typically masculine fashion he made the necessary adjustment. He found legitimate, enjoyable lovemaking with his wife so satisfying that he was no longer tempted to look elsewhere.

One satisfied husband summed it up rather graphically when asked if he had ever been tempted to try extramarital experiences: "When you have a Cadillac in the garage, how can you be tempted to steal a Volkswagen off the street?"

Female attitudes have been changing for the good in this area in recent years. Formerly it was common for many wives to look upon the sex act as a "necessary part of marriage" or a "wifely duty to perform." Now an increasing number of women view it as a God-given means of enriching their relationships for a lifetime.

4. *It reduces friction in the home.* Another result of a satisfying relationship between a couple is that it tends to reduce minor irritations in the home. A sexually satisfied man is usually a contented man. It will not solve major problems — it will not repair a bent fender or compensate for overcharging the budget — but it does reduce minor irritations. Many a wife has commented, "My husband is easier to get along with when our love life is what it should be. The children's jangling does not get on his nerves so much, and he finds it easier to be patient with other people."

Most men do not realize that some of their unexplained irritations can often be traced to an unsatisfied sex drive, but a wise wife will remain alert to this possibility. Somehow the world looks better and his difficulties shrink to life-size when sexual harmony prevails. It is as though his hard work and the pressures of life are worth it all when he and his wife consummate their love properly.

More is involved in this than just the satisfaction of the glands. A man sacrifices a great deal when he gets married — or at least he thinks so. As a single man, he is rather carefree and unpressured. If he wishes to spend a night out with the boys, he doesn't have to give an account of his whereabouts or satisfy another person's interests. If he sees something he wants, he just buys it whether he can afford it or not. That all changes with marriage.

Furthermore, his carefree spirit must make place for the increasing weight of responsibility marriage uniquely places on him. A woman thinks about economics occasionally, but usually with limited, short-range deliberation. The husband, however, must go to bed with the mental awareness that he is the supporter of his family. He awakens in the morning with the thought, "I'd better do a good job today; my wife and kids are depending on me." Unless he learns early in life to commit his way unto the Lord, that can be a heavy load to carry.

A husband of weak character came home one evening and announced to his wife, "I'm moving out tonight; I don't want to be married any more." Our investigation revealed that he was not interested in anyone else, but he confessed, "I'd rather spend my evenings working on my racing car than on a second job to support a family." His wife admitted that their physical relationship had been minimal and that she had never shown any appreciation for the sacrifices he had made for the family. Realizing that her indifference may have contributed to his dissatisfaction and irritation, she pleaded with him, "Give me another chance, and I'll prove to you that marriage is worth whatever sacrifices we both have to make." Some women get that second chance and prove it — this one didn't. The husband went his own selfish way into irresponsibility, and both remained miserable.

5. *It provides life's most exciting experience.* The titanic emotional and physical explosion that culminates the act of marriage for the husband is easily the most exciting experience he ever enjoys, at least on a repeatable basis. At that moment all other thoughts are obliterated from his mind; every gland and organ of his body seems to reach a fevered pitch. He feels as if his blood pressure and temperature soar nearly to the point of

losing control. By this time his breathing accelerates and he groans in ecstasy as the pressure breaks forth with the release of semen into the object of his love. Words are inadequate to describe this fantastic experience. Although the aggressive nature of men finds them engaging in various exciting activities — we know ski jumpers, motorcycle racers, jet pilots, sky divers, and pro football players — they all agree that lovemaking heads the list.

A heart patient provided the best description of the meaning for a man of the act of marriage that we have yet heard. Warned by his doctor that any unnecessary physical exertion could kill him, he continued love relations with his wife. At times he endured a body-rending experience of shock afterward — his heart palpitating, his face losing its color, and his extremities turning cold and clammy. Sometimes it took one or two hours before he could even get off the bed. When I suggested he might kill himself some day in making love to his wife, he quickly responded, "I can't think of a better way to go!"

The most beautiful aspect of all this is that God created the experience for man to share only with his wife. If he loves and cherishes her the way God commands him, a warm and affectionate relationship will develop to enrich their entire married life; the exciting and pleasurable experience of mutual lovemaking will be shared several thousand times during their marriage.

Napoleon Hill, in his very practical book for businessmen, *Think and Grow Rich*, betrays a common misunderstanding of the male sex drive when he cautions salesmen to limit the expression of their sex drive because it will tend to demotivate them.[2] Nothing could be further from the truth. A sexually satisfied husband is a motivated man. Hill was probably a victim of the false notion characteristic of the past generation which held that sex demanded such a great expenditure of energy that it certainly must sap a man's strength. Unless he is speaking of an abnormal frequency of several times a day, his advice is simply not valid. A sexually frustrated man has a hard time concentrating, is prone to be edgy and harder to work with, and more important, finds it difficult to retain lasting goals. By contrast, the truly satisfied husband refuses to waste his business day on trivia; he wants each moment to count so he can get home to the wife and family who give all his hard work real purpose and meaning.

Two letters sent to "Dear Abby" less than ten days apart bring a chuckle but well illustrate our point. The first one, from an irate husband who complained about his wife's lousy housekeeping, admitted to one positive trait he liked: "She'll go to bed with me whenever I want." The second letter came from a salesman who asked Abby to tell the first man to be grateful for his marital blessings: "If I had a wife like that, I'd be motivated to make enough money to hire her a maid to clean the house!"

Marabel Morgan, author of *The Total Woman*,[3] suggests that a man has two things on his mind when he gets home at night — food and sex — and not always in that order.

SEX DRIVE AND THOUGHT LIFE

The most consistent spiritual problem faced by the average red-blooded Christian man relates to his thought life. The male sex drive is so powerful that sex often seems to be uppermost in his mind. Any man in military service can testify that 95 percent of a serviceman's off-duty conversation revolves around sex. Dirty jokes and stories punctuated by four-letter words become a constant verbal bombardment.

Shortly after he becomes a Christian, such a man is convicted by the Word of God and the Holy Spirit to change his thought patterns. Our Lord, of course, knew this universal male problem, for He admonished, "I say unto you that whosoever looketh on a woman to lust after her hath committed adultery with her already in his heart" (Matt. 5:28). Such mental adultery has probably brought more sincere men to spiritual defeat than any other single sin.

Many Christian women fail to understand this male problem, which is one reason they often adopt such scanty dress. If they realized the thought problems which their indecent exposure causes the average man, many of them would dress more modestly; but since they are not so sexually stimulated at the sight of a male body, they do not readily perceive the male response. I caught this message as a G.I. stationed at the Las Vegas Army Air Base. After nineteen days on K.P. I received what I anticipated to be the greatest duty assignment possible — sweeping out the Wac's barracks. To my dismay, after checking out the smallest whisk broom I could find, I found the barracks empty; all the women were working. I returned to the quartermaster for a regular-sized broom, but during the cleanup I became aware of something rather startling: not one nude male pinup picture appeared in the two decks of that facility. By contrast, the 197 men in our barracks sported 193 pinup pictures of girls! Not until the recent overemphasis on sex have women reflected an increasing problem in this area. But they apparently have to cultivate it; men get it by nature.

Another illustration that women seem to lack the visual lust problem occurred recently in our home. Looking through *Sports Illustrated*, I came upon a picture of Mr. America. As I was admiring his bulging biceps and rippling muscles, Bev came up behind me, saw what I was looking at, and spontaneously responded, "Ugh, how grotesque!" Women have their own brand of spiritual problems, but mental-attitude lust is seldom one of them.

We have reviewed all this to make an important point. A loving, sexually responsive wife can be a great asset to her husband in keeping his thought life pleasing to God. That is not to suggest that his victory in Christ is dependent upon his wife's behavior — that is never the case. In fact, God has promised to give a warm-blooded, affectionate man the grace to live with a cold, indifferent woman. But many a carnal Christian husband has used his wife's sexual rejection as an excuse to compound his spiritual defeat further by periods of mental-attitude lust.

A loving wife who understands her husband's temptations in this regard will restrain the desire to squelch his advances and, because she thinks more of his needs than her own tiredness, will give her love freely to him. Her reward will be his ready response to her mood, and together they can share the rapturous experience of married love.

Notes

[1] Catherine Parker Anthony, *Textbook of Anatomy and Physiology* (St. Louis: C. V. Mosby Co., 1963), p. 46.
[2] Napoleon Hill, *Think and Grow Rich* (Cleveland: Ralston Publishing Co., 1956), p. 274.
[3] Published by Fleming H. Revell, Old Tappan, N. J., 1973.

3

For Men Only

During the first decade of marriage most men are more aggressive sexually than their wives. This is not always true, of course, depending on their temperaments and the monthly cycle of the wife, but it does provide a useful generalization. We might more accurately observe that sex is instinctively the most universal drive in men during their first decade of marriage, whereas for women it is a potential appetite that can be cultivated.

The wise and loving husband will therefore learn as much as he can about this subject in order to bestow upon his bride the greatest lovemaking experiences possible for both her benefit and his own. The more he strives for her enjoyment, the more he will help to create in her a favorable and exciting attitude toward the relationship. And the more she enjoys it, the more she will welcome and take delight in it.

The following suggestions will guide husbands in helping to create in their brides a wholesome appetite for lovemaking:

1. *Learn as much as you can.* We have already alluded to Dr. Ed Wheat's observation that almost all of a man's natural instincts that bring him sexual satisfaction

are not what bring his wife satisfaction. Since skilled lovemaking is not instinctive, a wise husband will learn as much as he can from a reliable, Christian source. By studying carefully our chapter on sex education and the art of lovemaking, he can gain much of the basic information that every husband should know. In addition, we recommend that every couple send for Dr. Wheat's three-hour cassettes and listen to them together.[1] Since discovering these fine taped lectures, I have required prospective bridegrooms to listen to them alone just before the wedding and urged the couple to take the tapes with them on their honeymoon to listen together. The material is highly informative and inclusive; more than one hearing is necessary to absorb all the information presented. For the couple who has been married longer, listening together to these tapes will open lines of communication that enables them to discuss subjects that previously may have seemed too difficult or personal for discussion.

2. *Practice self-control.* The apostle Paul said, "Look not every man on his own things, but every man also on the things of others" (Phil. 2:4). The principle of unselfishly acting as a blessing to one's partner certainly applies to lovemaking. As a man your sexual needs can often be satisfied within a matter of seconds; your wife's situation is just the reverse. She begins more slowly, then gradually builds to her sexual climax. Most men who accuse their wives of being frigid because they cannot reach an orgasm are often themselves the problem. About the time she is really getting excited, her husband ejaculates and leaves her with a limp penis, thus denying her an opportunity for a satisfying climax in intercourse.

By what means can we solve this problem? The husband must learn to control ejaculation, which demands strong self-discipline and practice. Some have suggested that men during intercourse may profitably contemplate nonstimulating things — sports, business, or, as one husband said, "I think about paying the monthly bills." Be careful not to overdo it, but concentrate on something that will delay your ejaculation and give your wife sufficient time for her emotional buildup. Remember, she usually requires ten to fifteen minutes of manipulation, either with your hand or through intercourse, before she can climax. Add to that a stimulating period of foreplay, and you will find plenty of time to practice self-control. Certain techniques that enable a man to postpone his ejaculation will be dealt with in detail in chapter 10.

3. *Concentrate on your wife's satisfaction.* Since a woman's orgasm is much more complex than a man's, it takes her longer to learn this art. A wise husband will make his wife's satisfaction a major priority early in their marriage so they can both benefit from her accomplishment.

The modern research of Masters and Johnson has revealed some interesting feminine responses that a husband should understand. For instance, the intriguing creature known as his wife does not regard foreplay as "a warmup before the game" as men often do; rather, to her it is an integral part of the big game. No husband should rush this activity just because his instincts suggest it. Instead, he should be aware of the four phases his wife goes through in the lovemaking process. Then he can devote his attention to bringing her through each stage.

4. *Remember what arouses a woman.* The sight of his wife getting ready for bed is sufficient stimulation for most men to be ready for the act of marriage. By contrast, the wife at this point is probably only ready for bed! Why is this so? Because men are stimulated by sight, whereas women respond more to other things — soft, loving words and tender touch.

Although not registering on a decibel tester, the auditory mechanism of a woman seems uniquely responsive to the male voice. For instance, teenage girls are more actively stimulated to emit screams and groans at rock concerts than are their male escorts. Rarely does one hear a man say, "Her voice excites me," whereas it is common to hear a woman exclaim, "His voice turns me on!" That auditory mechanism can be likened to the thermostat on the wall of your home. Entering the house at night, you can turn her thermostat up by speaking reassuring, loving, approving, or endearing words. You can likewise turn her thermostat down through disapproval, condemnation, or insults. In such cases it is safe to conclude that the louder your voice, the more rapidly you turn her down. It is a wise husband who from the time he gets home from work until he goes to bed uses his voice and his wife's auditory receiver to turn her on consistently.

Many a wife can identify with Mary: "My husband criticizes me from the time he walks in the house at night until we go to bed, and then he cannot understand why I'm not interested in lovemaking. I'm just not made that way!" If only more husbands were alert to this strong influence on their partner's emotions!

A woman's verbal receiver responds not only to the tone of voice, but to the message of the words. One couple requested help regarding the wife's "frigidity problem." After seven years of marriage, they shared three children and claimed mutual love and respect. Upon questioning, we discovered that he spoke lovingly to his wife, wooed her tenderly, and gained a warm response up to a point. Then suddenly she would turn "cold as ice." Eventually we discerned that his language was the culprit. In the heat of lovemaking excitement, he would introduce crude terms and crass expressions he had picked up in the army, forgetting that women tend to be more delicate in their word selections and often cannot understand why men use such uncouth speech to describe the beautiful things. To solve that "frigidity problem," he had only to learn better terminology. Such things are important to women.

5. *Protect her privacy.* Men are far more inclined than women to be sex braggarts. Many a thoughtless man has spoiled a vital relationship by indiscreetly revealing

his wife's intimate secrets to his buddies. If such a thing gets back to his wife, she feels betrayed. Such impropriety is not worth the risk. The beauty and sanctity of the intimate relationship you share is strictly confidential. Keep it that way.

6. *Beware of offensive odors.* The power of smell is one of our primary senses. Unfortunately some people experience more difficulty in this area than others, but today there is little excuse for bad breath, body odor, or any other offensive smells. A thoughtful lover will prepare for lovemaking by taking frequent baths, using effective deodorant, and practicing good oral hygiene.

On the subject of odors we share an observation made in the counseling room about extremely sensitive men. A melancholic man is a perfectionist, a very sensitive idealist. Consequently he may become "turned off" by the odors emitted by his wife's natural vaginal fluids. Women have a problem unshared by men, for the strong odor of a man's seminal fluid is usually not detected because it remains inside him until he ejaculates it into his wife's vagina, where it is not easily detected until after the resolution phase. But for the wife to permit penile entrance, she must secrete a vaginal lubricant that usually gives off an odor. A husband should simply learn to disregard that odor.

One such melancholic husband strongly complained that such an odor "turns me off so much that I cannot maintain my erection." Taking note of his limited sex education, I took the time to explain the function of his wife's vagina during sexual arousal. After convincing him this was a normal procedure over which his wife had no control, I concluded, "You should recognize that odor as the smell of love. Your wife's response to your love causes the lubricant to flow in anticipation of coitus with you; therefore you are the one causing the odor." With a sheepish grin he conceded, "I never thought of it that way." He later indicated that the "smell of love" concept had transformed their love life.

53

7. *Don't rush lovemaking.* Occasionally, when an experienced wife's monthly cycle causes her to be unusually passionate at a time when coitus is convenient, you both may sustain exciting orgasms in a matter of two minutes or less. When it happens, enjoy it — but don't expect it to be the norm. Most couples find that time in loveplay is a major key to feminine response. Therefore the husband who would be a good lover will not advance too quickly, but will learn to enjoy loveplay. He will not only wait until his wife is well-lubricated, but reserve his entrance into her vagina until her inner lips are engorged with blood and swollen at least twice their normal size.

The time spent in lovemaking varies with the culture. Researchers have indicated that the average experience runs from two minutes in some cultures to thirty minutes in others. Their comparisons suggest that the more a culture is masculine oriented and views sex as existing purely for male satisfaction, the shorter the time spent in the experience. In such a case, wives view it as a wife's "duty" or as an unpleasant function of life. In cultures where women are cherished and their satisfaction is sought, lovemaking is a time-consuming art.

A wise husband will keep in mind that his wife usually requires ten to fifteen minutes more time to reach her satisfaction than he does, but he will reckon it time well spent. Once he understands that a woman's nature ignites slowly and that her sexual tension increases gradually, he will cooperate with her needs.

8. *Communicate freely.* Most Christian women go into marriage relatively uninformed about sex and often retain the naive idea that their husbands know it all and will teach them. Rarely has she anticipated the fact that discussion of their intimate relations is difficult for most men. In fact, it is frequently the most difficult subject with which a couple has to cope. Consequently those who are most in need of the free-flowing expression of ideas on the subject practice it least.

I have been appalled to learn that even well-educated people find it difficult to discuss their love lives frankly. But this explains why couples get embarrassed when their children ask questions about sex — they have never been able to communicate with one another on the subject. An engineer married to a school teacher for ten years reported, "After all this time my wife still doesn't know what turns me on." When I asked, "Have you ever told her?" he replied, "No, I find it embarrassing to talk about sex. Besides, I think she should know." He was surprised when I responded, "How should she? You're different. You feel and react differently than a woman, and you possess an entirely different reproductive apparatus. Who did you think was going to tell her?" Most young brides expect their husbands to inform them of male needs. Unfortunately this does not usually happen. We have found that open communication between a husband and wife remains the best possible sex education. After all, a young bride does not need to know how man functions; she must simply learn to recognize the sexual responses of one. Who best can teach her about his needs but the object of her love — her husband?

9. *Love your wife as a person.* No human being likes to be considered an object, for in the quest for identity, everyone wants to be accepted as a person. A young man wins the affection of a young woman because he loves her as a person, showering his attention and affections upon her. After the wedding he too often becomes involved in business and work while his wife is busy raising their children. The two gradually become preoccupied with activities that do not include each other. Consequently the wife soon feels that the only thing they share is their bedroom life. That is always unacceptable to a woman. This is what gives rise to the complaint often heard in the counseling room, "The only time my husband is interested in me is when he wants sex"; or "I am no longer a person to my husband; I am just a sex object"; or "When my husband and I have relations, I don't feel it is a natural expression of love. Instead, I feel used."

It is interesting that when confronted with the wife's discontent, most husbands admit the validity of her complaint. But they are mystified at how it occurred so gradually, and they are not always sure what to do to correct it.

There are many things a man can do to express his love for his wife as a person. As he does, he will find them mutually therapeutic. Such expressions not only reassure his wife of his love, but also reaffirm it in his own heart. The little thoughtful things that he does or does not do confirm to his wife's heart that he loves her as a person.

For example, when a man comes home at night, he should indicate a personal interest in her and what she has been doing during the day, rather than become obsessed with the sports page, what is cooking for dinner, or what is on TV. In the evening, giving a hand with the children, relieving her of some of the responsibilities she has borne all day, is a further expression of his love. His spending time with the children rather than being enslaved by the boob tube does as much for the wife as it does for the children.

Moreover, a weekly night out for dinner away from the children is vitally important to the wife, even though the husband's yearnings may be for a quiet evening at home. Then occasionally there are those little birthday and holiday remembrances and, most of all, verbalized expressions of love and approval all through the evening.

A man who treats his wife as someone very special will usually find her eagerly responding to his expressions of love. When his words and actions together convince her that he dearly loves her, their intimate lovemaking is the natural, culminating expression of that love.

God had a wise plan in establishing one man for one woman. It is impossible for a man to love a woman as a person when there is another woman involved. A close friend shared that beautifully with me at lunch one day. We were discussing my Sunday sermon on King David. I asserted that I could not understand why a fifty-year-old man with twenty wives would stoop to committing adul-

56

tery with Bathsheba. Jim surprised me by saying, "I can understand that. David had so many wives he never knew what it was to have one true love."

God designed the beauty of marriage to be a lifetime of sharing experiences with one true love. As long as a man convinces his wife that their lovemaking is the expression of the true love he has for her, he will find her a willing and cooperative partner.

Notes

[1] Ed Wheat, M.D., "Sex Problems and Sex Technique in Marriage," available from Bible Believers Cassettes, 130 N. Spring, Springdale, AR 72764.

Bibliography

Andelin, Aubrey P. *Man of Steel and Velvet*. Santa Barbara, Calif.: Pacific Press Santa Barbara, 1972.

Anthony, Catherine Parker. *Textbook of Anatomy and Physiology*. St. Louis: C. V. Mosby Co., 1963.

Bird, Lewis P., and Reilly, Christopher T. *Learning to Love*. Waco, Tex.: Word Books, 1971.

Caprio, Frank S. *Sex and Love*. New York: The Citadel Press, 1965.

_____. *The Sexually Adequate Male*. Greenwich, Conn.: Fawcett Publications, 1951.

Chandler, Sandra S. *The Sensitive Woman*. Pasadena: Compass Press, 1972.

Clark, LeMon. *101 Intimate Sexual Problems Answered*. New York: New American Library, 1968.

Cooke, Charles E., and Ross, Eleanore. *Sex Can Be an Art!* Los Angeles: Sherbourne Press, 1964.

Curtis, Lindsay R. *Sensible Sex* (A Guide for Newlyweds). San Juan, Puerto Rico: Searle & Co., 1971.

Deutsch, Ronald M. *The Key to Feminine Response in Marriage*. New York: Random House, 1968.

Drakeford, John W. *The Great Sex Swindle*. Nashville: Broadman Press, 1966.

Ellzey, W. Clark. *How to Keep Romance in Your Marriage*. New York: Association Press, 1965.

Florio, Anthony. *Two to Get Ready*. Old Tappan, N.J.: Fleming H. Revell Co., 1974.

Greenblat, Bernard R. *A Doctor's Marital Guide for Patients*. Chicago: Budlong Press, 1964.

Hamilton, Eleanor. *Sex Before Marriage*. New York: Meredith Press, 1969.

Jones, H. Kimball. *Toward a Christian Understanding of the Homosexual*. New York: Association Press, 1966.

Levin, Robert, and Levin, Amy. "Sexual Pleasure: The

Surprising Preferences in 100,000 Women." *Redbook* 145 (September, 1970).

Masters, William H., and Johnson, Virginia E. *Human Sexual Response*. Boston: Little, Brown and Co., 1966.

Miles, Herbert J. *Sexual Happiness in Marriage*. Grand Rapids: Zondervan Publishing House, 1967.

Mumford, Bob. *Living Happily Ever After*. Old Tappan, N.J.: Fleming H. Revell Co., 1973.

Petersen, J. Allan, ed. *The Marriage Affair*. Wheaton, Ill.: Tyndale House Publishers, 1971.

Piper, Otto A. *The Biblical View of Sex and Marriage*. New York: Charles Scribner's Sons, 1960.

Rainer, Jerome, and Rainer, Julia. *Sexual Pleasure in Marriage*. New York: Pocket Books, 1959.

Reuben, David. *Any Woman Can!* New York: David McKay Co., 1971.

————. *Everything You Always Wanted to Know About Sex*. New York: David McKay Co., 1969.

————. *How to Get More Out of Sex*. New York: David McKay Co., 1974.

Rice, Shirley. *The Christian Home: A Woman's View*. Norfolk: Norfolk Christian Schools, 1965.

————. *Physical Unity in Marriage: A Woman's View*. Norfolk: Norfolk Christian Schools, 1973.

Robinson, Marie N. *The Power of Sexual Surrender*. New York: New American Library, 1962.

Scanzoni, Letha. *Sex and the Single Eye*. Grand Rapids: Zondervan Publishing House, 1968.

————. *Sex Is a Parent Affair*. Glendale, Calif.: Gospel Light Publications, 1973.

Sheridan, Edward P., and Sheridan, Kathleen, eds. *28 Experts View the Sexual Marriage*. Huntington, Ind.: Our Sunday Visitor, 1974.

Smith, Bob. *Love Story . . . the Real Thing*. Staff research at Peninsula Bible Church, Palo Alto, Calif., 1974.

Strong, James. "Dictionary of the Words in the Greek Testament" in *Strong's Exhaustive Concordance of*

Words in the Greek Testament. New York: Abingdon-Cokesbury Press, 1890.

Subak-Sharpe, Genell J. "Is Your Sex Life Going Up in Smoke?" *Reader's Digest*, 106 (January, 1975).

Thayer, Joseph Henry. *Thayer's Greek-English Lexicon of the New Testament*. Marshalltown, Del.: National Foundation for Christian Education, 1885, revised edition, 1889.

Timmons, Tim. *One Plus One*. Washington, D.C.: Canon Press, 1974.

Vincent, M.O. *God, Sex and You*. Philadelphia: J.B. Lippincott Co., 1970.